TIMOTHY BROWN IS A BAD BOY

MARY PAGE-CLAY

Archway Publishing books may be ordered through booksellers or by contacting:

Archway Publishing
1663 Liberty Drive
Bloomington, IN 47403
www.archwaypublishing.com
1 (888) 242-5904

Because of the dynamic nature of the Internet, any web addresses or links contained in this book may have changed since publication and may no longer be valid. The views expressed in this work are solely those of the author and do not necessarily reflect the views of the publisher, and the publisher hereby disclaims any responsibility for them.

Any people depicted in stock imagery provided by Getty Images are models, and such images are being used for illustrative purposes only.
Certain stock imagery © Getty Images.

ISBN: 978-1-4808-6941-7 (sc)
ISBN: 978-1-4808-6942-4 (e)

Print information available on the last page.

Archway Publishing rev. date: 01/06/2020

Dedication Page

Educational Colleagues

I dedicate this book to all the wonderful teachers and administrators that I have worked with during my teaching and administrative career for over the past 50 year. They are: Wake County Pubic Schools in Raleigh, North Carolina (Bugg and Washington Elementary Schools) – A special thanks to the staff at Bugg where I served as principal. You will always have a special place in my heart.

I also thank the following other schools that also contributed to my growth as an educator.

Elizabeth Vaughan Elementary in Woodbridge, VA

Carver Elementary School in District 11, Colorado Springs, Colorado

Lansing Elementary School in Lansing, Kansas

Department of Defense Schools in Augsburg and Kaiserslautern, West Germany

Eastside Elementary School, Saint Pauls, NC

Thank you to a special group of educators who gave me support and advice when I needed it most. They are: Danny Barnes, Pat Donahue, Marion Evans, Jarcelyn Hart, Allen Haymon, Christine Holston, Lillie Jesse, Jan Kidwell, Julye Mizelle, Linda Reynolds, Jean Sculati, Allynna Stone, Wiladean Thomas, Amy White, Debbie Wynn and Rachel Zeigler.

Students:

I am so thankful for the students who have been in the schools where I worked as a teacher or principal. You hold a special place in my heart. I miss those wonderful smiles and hugs. Without my interactions with you I would not have developed into the teacher that I became. Thank you- Boys and Girls!

Family
I also dedicate this book to my family:

Children: Dereck, Tracey, Melania, Marla –My #1 Supporters.

Grandchildren: Fautimon, Brandon, Rory, and Zoe

My Editor/ and Niece: Nicole Bell

Spouses:
Col. Gene Page (deceased) -He encouraged me to write. He also purchased my first computer.

Franklin Clay – a special thanks to Franklin for his continuous encouragement, feedback, and "listening ears".

Artist – Sonja Bot- Thank you for a job well done!

* If I missed your name, please forgive me. Please chalk it up to "old age". I love you!!

ABOUT THE AUTHOR

Mary Page-Clay is a retired school administrator with over 40 years of experience in elementary schools across the United States and American Dependent Schools in West Germany. As a classroom teacher she developed a passion to reach children who were not excited about learning and did not feel supported by their teachers.

The situations in this book were inspired by real events that still occur in classrooms across the world today. Mary admits that it's not easy to reach every child but she still believes that most people teach because they love children and want to inspire each generation to love learning. This book is designed to be used in elementary schools for staff development and includes a guide book with activities for large and small group training.

Mary still loves teaching and volunteers at a public school in Colorado Springs, where she lives with her husband. Her other books include "Preacher's Coming to Dinner" and "The Mouse in the House".

ABOUT THE ARTIST

Sonja Bot has been a freelance illustrator for 5 years, infusing her distinct style into an array of formats, including textiles and advertisements. During her time teaching in China, she observed that students of all ages learned quickly when they were engaged by captivating imagery along with a great storyline, and education is now an important part of her design work and art. "Timothy Brown is a Bad Boy" is her first foray into the adventurous and fun world of children's book illustration.

The first day of school started the same as usual.
I waited by the door of my third grade classroom
To greet each child as they walked in.
Many parents came to meet me, their child's new teacher.
Everything would have been just wonderful,
If on my list I had not seen the dreaded name of Timothy Brown.
He was a teacher's nightmare.
Timothy Brown was a bad boy.

1

He walked into my classroom
As if he owned the place.
That unruly hair had not been combed.
His clothes were clean but threadbare.

"Hi ya, Teacher," he greeted me with a grin.
"Good morning, Timothy," I said coolly.
"Welcome to my classroom," I stiffly added.
I could see that Timothy Brown was still a bad boy.

2

He had his mother with him.

She was a sad looking woman with brown skin and long, fuzzy braids.

She smiled as she shook my hand.

"I don't work regularly so I can come in to help," she offered.

"How nice, but we have all the help we need," I replied.

"If things change, I will call you," I added with a smile.

She nodded her head as she kissed Timothy goodbye.

3

I felt a little guilty.

I could always use more help.

However, Timothy's mother would be the last one I would call.

My other parents wouldn't approve.

She probably wasn't educated and didn't dress properly.

I certainly wouldn't ask her to tutor a student.

What could the mother of Timothy Brown do for my class?

Timothy had difficulty learning and was reading below grade level.
When I tested my students for reading, he was the lowest in the class.
So I decided to let him read by himself.
I also let him play on the computer during reading time.
That way I could help students who wanted to be helped.
I did not have time to waste on a boy with a bad attitude.

Timothy always raised his hand during class.

Most of the time, I ignored him because I knew that he didn't know the answer.

I pretended I did not see him and I called on someone who could answer the question.

Timothy was not a good reader, however he seemed to like math,

But he never finished the whole page of problems.

He also misbehaved during group work and I frequently had to move him.

Most of the students did not want to work with him anymore.

But I wasn't surprised because Timothy Brown was a bad boy.

We went on a class field trip.
This time we went ice skating.
Timothy didn't bring in his money, and I did not let him skate.
According to the principal, I still had to take him with me.

Another teacher offered to pay for him but I refused the offer!
I could tell that she was upset.
But Timothy had to learn, no money, no fun!
Besides, Timothy Brown was a bad boy.

We were going to put on a special third grade play.
I had to choose the students who were going to speak.
I told the class they could try out for special parts.
Well, that Timothy Brown tried out for Robin Hood.
To my surprise, he did well!
But I needed someone who looked like Robin Hood.
Robin Hood didn't have brown skin and wooly hair.

8

Timothy asked, "Teacher, can I be Robin Hood?"
I smiled and politely said,
"Well Timothy, the speaking parts are long,"
"You might have problems memorizing so much."
"But I can do it, Teacher, I promise I can," he pleaded.
"Timothy, we really do need someone who looks like Robin Hood."
I ignored the tears running down his face because I knew,
Timothy Brown was a bad boy.

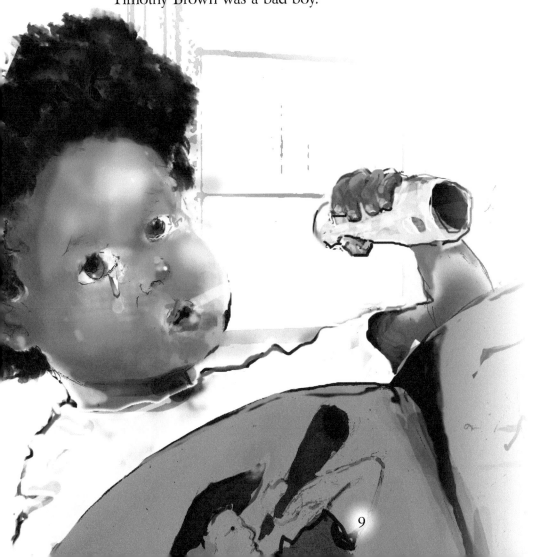

9

Little Michael Cummings was the perfect Robin Hood
With his fair skin and light brown hair.
His mother helped him learn all the lines.
I felt so proud when he knew them from memory.
I had to do what was best for the class
So I let Timothy sing in the chorus.
He had a nice voice and he sang loudly.
However, I couldn't forget that Timothy Brown was a bad boy.

I tried so hard with that boy.
Sometimes I even let him be a helper,
That didn't make him act any better.
When I called on him in class, I knew he didn't know the answer,
So I quickly called on another student
Like little Emily Holt with her long, black curls.
That proper little lady always tried to help Timothy.

I can tell you that on most days, Timothy pushed my buttons.

One day he tried to tell me that someone had taken his math book.

He wanted me to give him another one.

His mother even wrote me a note asking for another book,

As if I would believe anything that Timothy had to say.

Well, I did not give him another book.

Who was going to pay for it? Where would his mother get the money?

It would be a waste because Timothy Brown was a bad boy.

Can Timmy have a new math book please? Sorry he misplaced his.

Thank you,
Mrs. Brown

12

Timothy wanted to be line leader.
I told him that he could not be a leader until his attitude improved.
"I'll be good," he promised.
I knew better but I decided to give him a chance.

He was line leader for one day!
He tripped another student.
"He called me a name," Timothy explained.
I didn't believe him because Timothy Brown was a bad boy.

Almost everyone in class brought in eggs for our Easter egg hunt.

Everyone except Timothy, that is. That was the last straw.

"No eggs, no hunt!" I yelled at that boy.

It wasn't fair for the other students to have to share.

"I wanted to be in the hunt but the eggs were all gone," Timothy cried.

His mother should have gone out to buy more eggs.

"Too bad, Timothy!" I answered.

Everyone took turns bringing in snacks for the class.
I knew Timothy would forget to bring his snack
So I never sent the note home with him.
"Why can't I have a snack day?" he asked.
"Don't worry, Timothy. We have enough snacks already."
He didn't like that one little bit.
But what else should I expect from him?

Snacks

mon Madeline
tues Jon
wed Gabriel
thur Sa
fri R
mon Sim
Harri
Owen

15

On warm days we went outside to play.

However, most of the time Timothy Brown had to watch

Because he didn't get his morning seatwork completed.

He went outside with the class but he couldn't play.

The older boys from fourth and fifth grades always inquired,

"Can Timothy play with us today?"

"Not until he finishes his work," I replied.

He didn't deserve to play because Timothy Brown was a bad boy.

As the year progressed, things got worse day after day.

Timothy started coming to school late.

He harassed the other students.

He scribbled all over his papers.

There was no more "Good morning, Teacher."

He just stomped through the door.

He didn't seem to care, but I expected it.

One day, the principal came in to observe.

He watched Timothy and even stopped to talk to him.

Timothy answered his questions.

The next day, the principal called me to his office.

"What's wrong with Timothy Brown?" he asked.

"His test scores have all gone down since the beginning of the year."

"He's really not very bright," I pointed out.

I really tried to help that boy.
I did all that I could to be fair.
I tried to include him in class discussions
But he would just stare at me.
One day he asked if he could talk to the counselor.
Well, I was having none of that!
He just wanted to be out of the classroom.

19

One day his mom came in for a conference.

"Timothy isn't happy here," she said in a small voice.

"I don't know why. Timothy gets along well with most people," she added.

"But he really should be in Special Education classes," I answered.

"I don't want him there," she said bravely.

"Well, he will just always be behind," I said angrily.

What else could anyone expect?

Obviously, his mother was in denial.

I noticed that Timothy smiled at the teacher next door.
She always asked me how he was doing.
Why should she care, with her blue eyes and blonde hair?
One day she gave Timothy a book to read.
He was sitting in class reading the book but I made him return it.
He had not even finished his morning seatwork!
I told her not to interfere with my students.

I was happy when the year ended.
Timothy would be a problem for someone else.
I even heard that the teacher next door had asked for him.
Poor thing! "Do you know what you are doing?" I asked.
"Timothy deserves a chance," she said.
I shrugged my shoulders and walked away.
She'll be sorry, I thought. "Don't call me," I said with a smile.
Because I knew and she would soon find out that . . .

TIMOTHY

BROWN

IS

A

BAD

BOY!

23

NOTES

NOTES

NOTES

TIMOTHY BROWN IS A BAD BOY

BY MARY PAGE-CLAY

GROUP DISCUSSION GUIDE

OVERVIEW

Administrators should read the entire guide before planning the first large group session. Notes for each session are broken into four parts:

Prepare for the session – The Administrator and his or her Leadership Team should make any necessary arrangements before each large group session.

Opening the discussion – The Administrator opens the large group meeting, sets context, and facilitates open and honest sharing among attendees.

During the discussion – The facilitator uses sample questions to engage the group and encourage discussion. The scribe captures observations and lessons learned.

Closing the discussion – The scribe shares his or her notes from the session. The facilitator closes the session and assigns activities for the group to complete before the next session.

MATERIALS

You'll need the following materials for each session.

- Whiteboards or flip charts – Use in large and small groups to capture key learnings. Provide enough for each small group to have at least one.
- Journals or notebooks – Provide enough for each participant to have at least one.
- Pens, pencils, and markers –Participants use to capture notes in their journals. Scribes use to write information on the whiteboards or flipcharts.
- Food – Provide a light meal or snacks for each session. You may also provide a celebratory meal during the final large group discussion.
- Music – Use music as a transition prompt and to celebrate during the final large group session.

ROLES AND RESPONSIBILITIES

Responsibilities	Principal or Designated Leader
Facilitate open discussion among attendees.	• Read the entire guide before scheduling the first large group session. • Invite all staff members who work with children. • Provide suggested materials. • Set context for each session. • Open and close the large group sessions. • Facilitate open discussion among staff. • Be visible and available to address questions and observe the shared experiences of group members. • Partner with the Leadership Team to identify opportunities for improvement.
Leadership Team	• Attend as many sessions as possible. • Capture notes from large group discussions. • Collaborate with small group scribes to compile session notes in preparation for the final large group session. • Be visible and available to address questions and observe the shared experiences of the group members. • Partner with the Administrator to identify opportunities for improvement.

Responsibilities	• Principal or designated leader will facilitate discussion among attendees
Small Group Facilitator	• Read *Timothy Brown Is a Bad Boy* at the opening of each session. • Facilitate the discussion. • Identify patterns and commonalities. • Share insights with the large group.
Small Group Scribe	• Capture relevant notes to share with the small group and large group. • Share notes with Leadership Team, if necessary.
Small Group Timekeeper	• Ensure the group adheres to the schedule for each session.
Designated Staff Member	• Share personal classroom or student challenges and successes. • Come prepared to have an open and honest discussion with peers and leadership. • Identify opportunities for improvement in the classroom and the school.

LARGE GROUP SESSION ONE

Prepare for the Session
Administrator and Leadership Team

Assess the needs of the large group during staff meetings or one-on-one discussions, and then meet with your Leadership Team to decide how you will address opportunities for improvement.

- Are your students performing at defined academic levels?
- Are students participating in class discussions and activities?
- Is there open dialogue between students and teachers?

Open the Discussion
Administrator

- Set context and ground rules for the workshop. For example, everyone should participate, turn off cell phones, stay within the group and please avoid side conversations.
- Share how long each session will run and share dates for future gatherings.
- Provide a timeline for the day's activities.
- Encourage the staff to have open and honest discussions in group settings.

During the Discussion
Leadership Team

- Create an environment where the group feels comfortable sharing their ideas and opinions. Inform teachers that information shared during the sessions is confidential and should not be discussed outside of the group setting.
- Read *Timothy Brown Is a Bad Boy* to the group.

- ○ The Administrator and members of the Leadership Team should share their thoughts about the book to kick off the large group discussion.
- ○ Encourage attendees to share their initial reactions to the book.

- At this introduction to the book you may ask sample questions to prepare attendees for discussions in their small groups.

Sample Questions

Ask questions that you think will motivate your staff to discuss specific situations in their classrooms. Encourage your staff members to discuss the book within small groups and be prepared to share their insights when the large group reconvenes.

Questions will vary in following sessions and should be based on the feedback of the group.

- What are your initial reactions to Timothy Brown?
- Do you know parents who remind you of Timothy's mother?
- Do you have any students in your class who remind you of Timothy? If so, how do you communicate with these students?
- Describe the teacher – her beliefs, perceptions, personality.
- What could the teacher do to change her relationship with Timothy?

Transition to Small Groups

After a few minutes of open discussion provide instructions for the small group breakout sessions.

- Limit the size of groups to no more than eight participants.
- Ask each group to choose a facilitator, timekeeper, and scribe.
- Encourage attendees to take personal notes in the journals you provided for them.

- Remind groups to be prepared to share their findings when the large group reconvenes.
- Restate the timeframe for small group discussion.

Close the Discussion
Administrator

After the small group session ends bring the group together and ask the facilitator or a representative from each group to share findings from their small group's discussion.

- Ask the speaker to share any insights, strategies or thoughts about the book.
- Have a member of your Leadership Team capture the groups' feedback and key discussion points. You may use these notes to plan for the next large group session or to consider change management in your school.

Before dismissing for the day be sure to thank your staff for their willingness to share openly and honestly about their challenges, successes, and opportunities for improvement.

Assign any takeaways for the group and provide the date of the next group session.

Follow a similar format for each large group discussion.

SMALL GROUP SESSION ONE

Open the Discussion
Facilitator

- Read the book and kick-off the discussion.
- Remind the scribe to take notes on the whiteboard or flipchart.
- Set a time limit for the first question and ask the timekeeper to begin monitoring the time.

During the Discussion
Facilitator

Questions are in random order. Select questions that will encourage your group to have a productive discussion.

Sample Questions

✓ On day one Timothy Browns walks into the classroom with a negative attitude. What could the teacher have done on the first day to begin changing his attitude?
✓ Why did the teacher have a negative opinion about Timothy even though she did not know him?
✓ What is the one thing that happened to Timothy that touched you – positively or negatively?
✓ Why did the teacher assume that Timothy's mother had little education?
✓ What assumptions have you made about your students and their parents?
✓ Do you agree with Timothy's reading instruction? What could the teacher have done instead of putting him in a group by himself?
✓ Are there resources available at your school for students who are struggling with reading or math? *If so, have you referred your struggling students to a specialist and are parents involved?*

Close the Discussion
Facilitator and Scribe

A few minutes before the close of the discussion ensure that the scribe has captured all notes and relevant talking points.

- Give the group time to write in their journals.
- Ask the scribe to review the key discussion points from the session.
- Assign activities to the group to be completed before the next session.

Assignment

For the next session, ask each group member to:

- Be prepared to bring information about a student who is struggling academically or emotionally in their classroom and share the strategies he or she is using to facilitate change.
- Be open to positive suggestions from the other members of the group.
- Apply the lessons learned from the group discussion and share any changes in the behavior of their students.

The facilitator should be prepared to share the findings of the group.

Follow this same format for each small group discussion.

LARGE GROUP SESSION TWO

Prepare for the Session
Administrator and Leadership Team

Speak with staff members and ask about strategies they're using in the classroom to improve student's behavior. Ask them to share any positive feedback they've received from parents. Be prepared to share your findings during the session.

Open the Discussion
Administrator

- Welcome the staff to the second large group session.
- Share with the group any progress you've observed. Identify specific students who have made noticeable improvements in their behavior or academics.
- Share any letters or special notes from parents about their child's improvements.

During the Discussion
Leadership Team

- Invite facilitators to share their findings from the first small group session.
- Ask a participant from each small group to share information about a student who is struggling academically or emotionally. Encourage him or her to share the strategies they're using to facilitate change.
- Ask a participant from each small group to share success stories. Encourage him or her to share specific information such as test scores, parent letters, feedback from a specialist, and classroom awards or citations.
- Ask specialist staff to share any improvements they've observed with students in their classes.
- To encourage discussion, you may ask sample questions to prepare attendees for small groups.

Sample Questions

Ask questions that you think will motivate your staff to discuss specific situations in their classrooms. Encourage your staff members to discuss the book within their small groups and prepare to share when the large group reconvenes.

Questions will vary in the following sessions and should be based on the feedback of the group..

- How would you handle a new student with behavior problems who comes into the classroom at mid-year?
- What would you do if you had a colleague who was unable to bond with a student who had problems similar to Timothy Brown?
- Would you let this relationship continue all year without interceding in some way?
- How would you help a fellow teacher bring out the best in Timothy?
- What would you do if Timothy was the child of another teacher in the school? Would you treat him differently?

Transition to Small Groups

After a few minutes of open discussion, provide instructions for the small group breakout sessions.

- Encourage the attendees to take personal notes in the journals you provided for them.
- Remind groups to be prepared to share their findings when the large group reconvenes.
- Restate the timeframe for small group discussion.

Close the Discussion
Administrator

After the small group session ends bring the group together and ask the facilitator or a representative from each group to share findings from their small group's discussion.

- Remind the group that the goal of the discussion is to inspire them to think about their relationship with their students.
- Ask the facilitators to share any insights, strategies or thoughts about the book.
- Have a member of your Leadership Team capture the groups' feedback and key discussion points. You may use these notes to plan for the next large group session or to consider change management in your school.

Before dismissal, be sure to thank your staff for their willingness to share openly and honestly about their challenges, successes, and opportunities for improvement.

Assign any takeaways for the group and provide the date of the next group session.

Follow a similar format for each large group discussion.

SMALL GROUP SESSION TWO

Open the Discussion
Facilitator

- Read *Timothy Brown Is a Bad Boy* and kick-off the discussion.
- Remind the scribe to take notes on the whiteboard or flipchart.
- Set a time limit for the first question and ask the timekeeper to begin monitoring the time.
- Before you select a sample question, ask if anyone would like to share any differences in their approach to teaching since session one.

During the Discussion
Facilitator

Questions are in random order. Select questions that will encourage your group to have a productive discussion.

Sample Questions

- Do you think the teacher should have taken Timothy skating even though he did not pay?
    - Was it fair to punish him for something that he could not control?
    - How do you handle class trips when there are students who cannot pay?
    - Do you keep this as a private matter between you and the student or do you embarrass him in front of the other students?
- Did the other students think Timothy was a bad boy?
- Should the teacher embarrass Timothy in front of the other students?
    - Should knowledge of previous behavior affect your treatment of the student?
- Why did the teacher ignore Timothy's request to be in the play? Should she have given him a chance?

- Why did the teacher refuse to allow Timothy to participate in the Easter egg hunt?
- If Timothy's mom were the PTA president or another teacher in the school, would Timothy have been treated the same? Are you more respectful of some students because of their parents' station in life?
- How did Timothy's teacher feel about the teacher who gave Timothy positive attention?

Close the Discussion
Facilitator and Scribe

A few minutes before the close of the discussion ensure that the scribe has captured all notes and relevant talking points.

- Give the group time to write in their journals.
- Ask the scribe to review the key discussion points from the session.
- Assign activities to complete before the next session.

Assignment

For the next session, ask each group member to:
- Choose one student who is making a positive change academically and behaviorally in their classroom.
- Be prepared to share the behaviors and strategies used to help the student change their behavior.

Follow this same format for each small group discussion.

LARGE GROUP SESSION THREE

Prepare for the Session

- One to two weeks before the session, distribute a questionnaire to the staff and inform them that the Leadership Team will summarize and share the results during the large group celebration. You may use the following questions or develop your own.
  - How did *Timothy Brown is a Bad Boy* affect the way you approach teaching?
  - Which incident in the book had the largest impact on your classroom management style? Why?
  - What are some of the positive changes taking place in your classroom and the strategies that you used to facilitate change?
  - Which strategies will you implement to strengthen your relationship with the parents of your students?
  - What will you do each morning to start your day in a positive manner?
- Before this session take time to speak to as many participants as possible. Identify teachers who are willing to share their success stories with the large group.

Before the Discussion
Administrator

- Welcome staff to the third large group session.
- Inform the group that this is the final large group session where they will be asked to share observations and things learned from the last session.

During the Discussion
Leadership Team

- Invite the teachers who are willing to share their stories to share with the large group.
- Encourage participants to share behaviors and the strategies he or she used to modify the student's behavior.

GROUP SHOULD WRITE IN THEIR JOURNALS

Transition to Small Groups

After a few minutes of open discussion, provide instructions for the small group breakout sessions.

- Encourage the attendees to take personal notes in the journals you provided for them.
- Remind groups to be prepared to share their findings when the large group reconvenes.
- Restate the timeframe for small group discussion.

Close the Discussion
Administrator

After the small group session ends bring the group together and ask the facilitator or a representative from each group to share findings from their small group's discussion.

- Remind the group that this is the last time they'll be asked to openly share insights, strategies or thoughts about the book. Let the group guide the discussion.
- Have a member of your Leadership Team capture the groups' feedback and key discussion points.
- Before dismissing for the day be sure to:
    o Thank your staff for their willingness to share openly and honestly about their challenges, successes, and opportunities for improvement.
    o Invite the staff to the upcoming large group celebration.

SMALL GROUP SESSION THREE

Before the Discussion
Facilitator

- Read *Timothy Brown Is a Bad Boy* and kick-off the discussion.
- Remind the scribe to take notes on the whiteboard or flipchart.
- Set a time limit for the first question and ask the timekeeper to begin monitoring the time.
- Before you select a sample question, ask if anyone would like to share any differences in their classroom or in a particular student since applying the strategies shared during session two.
- Ask each participant to share observations about a student that is making positive changes academically or behaviorally.

During the Discussion
Facilitator

Questions are in random order. Select questions that will encourage your group to have a productive discussion.

Sample Questions

✓ Do you have students who are not performing well academically? Are these students receiving extra help from a resource teacher or volunteer?

✓ Do you start each day with a positive attitude that will help your students work hard to have a successful school year? Share some of your strategies.

✓ When you watch your students interacting with their peers in the classroom, what do you see? Is it different for students with learning or behavior challenges?

✓ Do you have students who do not have any friends in your classroom? What can you do to change this?

GIVE GROUP TIME TO WRITE IN THEIR JOURNALS

Close the Discussion
Facilitator and Scribe

A few minutes before the close of the discussion ensure that the scribe has captured all notes and relevant talking points.

- Give the group time to write in their journals.
- Ask the scribe to review the key discussion points from the session.
- Remind the team that this is the final small group discussion.
- Thank attendees for their participation.

CELEBRATION!!

Prepare for the Celebration

- Provide food and music to celebrate.
- Review the questionnaire summary with the Leadership Team.
- Prepare to share your personal learnings.

Before the Celebration

Administrator

- Thank participants for their time and willingness to share their challenges, successes, and opportunities for improvement.

During the Celebration

Administrative, Leadership Team

- Create a festive environment and encourage the participants to informally share what they have learned from each other.
- Please give staff time to talk to their peers.
- Ask the Leadership Team to share the findings from the questionnaire.
- Share your final thoughts and lessons learned.
- Invite participants to share any final thoughts with the group.
- Kick-off the celebration!

Close the Celebration

- Thank participants for their time, energy, and participation.
- Consider identifying another book that will motivate your staff to keep looking for ways to support their students.

A NOTE FROM THE AUTHOR

Thank you for sharing this book with your staff. I'm proud that I had a chance to write a book that is so close to my heart. I taught school for many years and now that I'm retired I can look back and see the things that I did well and things that I wish I had done better.

Teaching is a tremendous responsibility and when you do the very best that you can, you will leave the profession with a sense of peace. I hope that the rest of your teaching years will be filled with flexibility, positive interactions, and love for your students and colleagues. Remember, it takes a village to teach a child.

Warmly,
Mary Page-Clay

NOTES

NOTES

Printed in the United States
By Bookmasters